"Sadie"

First Year In The Life & Adventures Of an American Water Spaniel

Robert (Bampa) and Grandma Darbie Baker

AuthorHouse™
1663 Liberty Drive
Bloomington, IN 47403
www.authorhouse.com
Phone: 833-262-8899

Because of the dynamic nature of the Internet, any web addresses or links contained in this book may have changed since publication and may no longer be valid. The views expressed in this work are solely those of the author and do not necessarily reflect the views of the publisher, and the publisher hereby disclaims any responsibility for them.

Any people depicted in stock imagery provided by Getty Images are models, and such images are being used for illustrative purposes only. Certain stock imagery © Getty Images.

This book is printed on acid-free paper.

ISBN: 979-8-8230-1531-8 (sc)
ISBN: 979-8-8230-1532-5 (e)

Library of Congress Control Number: 2023918606

Print information available on the last page.

Published by AuthorHouse 09/29/2023

authorHOUSE®

Sadie at 1 year

Sadie Quote
"Growing up a 'Baker' has a lot of fun challenges"

"Growing up doesn't mean I have to quit having fun. I love grabbing a towel, bathroom mat, baby blankets, hankie's, underwear, anything cloth, being stubborn, and doing these things because I like to have fun with my parents. The grab and catch is fun but when I give it back, I love it when my parents say, "good girl".

Thanks

*We want to thank all who're **not laughing at us** and those **who're not trying to make us feel bad** because we should "not have adopted a puppy". And thank those who have dogs and gave advice throughout our journey with this new pup. Thanks to all of you.*

Preface

We, (*Grandma Darbie and Bampa*), had been thinking about getting a dog ever since our cocker spaniel, *"Lady"*, passed on. Both of us had dogs most of our lives and know the value of a pet in our home. Over time, we did fairly good and remained *"dogless"* after Ladies passing for about 8 years. What we should have done was immediately adopt. We know that now. Instead, we took to dog sitting for a couple of neighbors and called it *"our dog fix"*. You ask yourself *"why should they adopt immediately"*? Everyone has different reasons, but ours *"was our age"*. You see, we're older (*retired*) and if we had adopted at that time, that dog would be around 7 years old now (*49 in dog years*) and would have already mellowed. Since we're not getting any younger, we now have one more thing to think about. And that *"thing"* is a puppy who seems to be "half *American Water Spaniel* and *half tornado"*. She's actually a full-blooded American Water Spaniel with a bundle of energy, and her breed is also a hunting dog. When we look at her and ask ourselves *"what did we do"*, we can't get past her eyes. It seems as if she's telling us *"**you adopted me!!!, and I stole your hearts**"*.

It was a little over a year ago when we were visiting a nephew in Arkansas and he had the cutest small (actually medium sized) dog that had the neatest personality, i.e., inquisitive, loyal, responded to commands, and an all-around good dog for his 4 kids. His dog *"Red"* is the neatest pet and it seemed the timing was right for us. We were ready to adopt and this was the breed we wanted. Yep, his dog was an *American Water Spaniel (and we weren't familiar with the breed)*, who at the time was about 9 months old.

This book is about two older individuals raising a puppy from *"the puppies point of view"*. The time and energy involved with raising a puppy is something we forgot about and since we're older, there was one key element we definitely had only experienced in small chunks and that was *"being a chew toy"*. Our kids had always been the chew toy, but now, we were and we have bruises and teeth marks to prove it. We wished there was a *"rent a kid"* business somewhere and we could have rented a couple for about 6 months. That would have taken care of the chew toy period of raising a puppy. At our age, our blood is thinner, our skin is thinner, our reflexes are less, and the only thing we tend to do quicker is lose our tempers.

The reason for this book is simple. During the process of raising Sadie, we took videos of her accomplishments and the fun we were having with the process and successes. We sent these to our great grandkids and they started looking forward to seeing those videos. When we sat down and looked at these videos, we noticed that Sadie was telling us a story. So, we put pen to paper and the result is this book. Hope you enjoy *"Sadie's"* story as much as we love living it.

Table of Contents

Chapter 1

Interesting Facts *(American Water Spaniels)*

Can you believe it, barely a year old and I get to author a book about my life. I know it might not be interesting to everyone, but I think it's exciting and it should be fascinating to some. But before I get to the good parts, thought I'd tell you about my *"breed of dog"*. I learned about most of these things from my dog parents and my human dad when he was reading facts to my mom. I hope every puppy gets to find out who they are and what they represent in their different breeds. Anyway, here comes the facts.

I am an *American Water Spaniel* **(AWS)** and we aren't well known outside the Great Lakes area of the United States. We are great dogs if you're living near water and you're outdoorsy. My human parents live in Arizona (*no, not near any water*), and at this time in their lives, they're not outdoorsy, but I do know they love me. Incidentally, I will be alternating between **American Water Spaniel** and (**AWS**) for purpose of not having to write the entire words all the time. Right now, the words are bigger than me, (at least longer).

We are a hunting dog breed that hunts all sorts of small game, and even though I haven't hunted yet, my dog parents told me that my breed specializes in waterfowl. I am a natural swimmer as well as a skilled retriever and hunter, my versatility allows me to perform in all sorts of the many dog sports and activities such as *agility, obedience trials, hunting tests, rallies, therapy (means I'm smart), tracking and search and rescue, as well as conformation.* My web feet help me in the swimming department, but I really haven't been in water where my feet don't touch the bottom. Now that I'm spayed, I can't compete in conformation shows, but there are plenty of other activities I can have fun with.

I don't know how much of this is a trait of my breed, but I have this desire to jump on people. Friends who come over on Sundays are always my targets. I will go more into this in Chapter 3.

I crave companionship, but I'm not bored and I know this because I don't feel I have to chew on things and be destructive. I have picked out some interesting things to chew on but it's a game between my parents and me. It also crosses into my breed "trait" of being stubborn, so every time I want attention, I just might do something I know is wrong, but I get a kick out of my human parents telling me to *"release or drop"*. Then they say, *"good girl"*.

I don't like harsh treatment because I can become timid or stubborn. I respond to *gentle touches* and training techniques that use rewards for getting it right, rather than punishment for getting it wrong. The longer I'm in this *"growing up period"*, the stubborn thing seems to get worse and now I think it's truly a *"trait"*. Sometimes I can't seem to stop myself. I see something I'd like to get attention with, and ***"boom"*,** I just do it.

My breed was developed in the Fox and Wolf River valleys of Wisconsin during the mid-1800's. I don't know anything about the 1800's, so I'm just relaying this information. All I can figure out is the 1800's seem like a long time ago. But everything prior to me being here is a long time ago. Remember, I'm not too old as of this writing. Reliable breeding records date back to 1865. The breeds that were thought to have been included in AWS development is the "**English Water Spaniel**", "**Irish Water Spaniel**", "**Curly Coated Retriever**", "**native Indian Dogs**", the "**Poodle**", and either the "**Sussex Spaniel**" or another type of field spaniel like a "**Springer Spaniel**". The hunting instincts have been bred out of a lot of these breeds, but still remains in the AWS and even today, they're used primarily for hunting. Being a smaller hunting dog, we make an excellent house pet as well and this is why my human parents wanted me.

I was bred to be medium-sized and I have a dense, curly coat that protects me from cold water as well as from briars in the woods. Being smaller, I can fit into a canoe, or little boat and tenderly retrieve grouse, quail, pheasant, and ducks. While hunting, I will remain close to my parents (*or whoever I'm hunting with*) rather than range. Doesn't this sound good, who wouldn't want me. All this and I make a good house pet. When you look at the pictures in this book, just look at my face. *I'm gorgeous*.

But I almost became extinct. When the larger retriever breeds from England became popular, my breed began to fall out of favor. Doctor F.J. Pfeifer of New London, Wisconsin, got busy and saved the AWS. He bred and sold AWS's, formed a breeding club and helped to develop a breed standard (*a written description of how the AWS should look*). He paved the way for the United Kennel Club's recognition of the breed in 1920, the Field Stud Book in 1938, and the American Kennel Club's recognition of the breed in 1940. One of his own dogs, **"Curly Pfeifer"**, was the first registered American Water Spaniel. Does that mean I'm related to him......Hmmmmm........."*just wondering*".

We remain a rare breed, with fewer than 3,000 registered in existence today. This by itself, saved the breed from splitting into two groups; one group used for dog show competitions, and the other to continue the breed's job as a hunting companion.

Since the AWS breed was developed in Wisconsin, it makes sense that we became the *"Wisconsin State Dog"* in 1986**.** That means I have the honor of being the *"State dog breed"* of Wisconsin and the word *"honor"* is a big word to live up to. Wow....All that and I'm stubborn, nosey, and full of energy. What else could my parents want.

I was lucky, my parents got me from a good breeder, one that was concerned about my future, spent a lot of time with me and my littermates, took us to the Vet, and had quite a questionnaire about my potential new parents. Because of this, my human parents have a lot to live up to and doggonit I'm sure they will. I like that word *"doggonit"*, it fits me.

Did I tell you about all the colors that my breed has. Almost any color you can imagine. My parents said our breed of dog should have been named after Henry Ford, the automobile builder. That's because you can get any color you want in an AWS as long as it's brown, or some shade of brown. Let's see, there's *"chocolate"*, *"liver"*, and *"reddish brown"*. I came out *"Chocolate"*, but my ears seem to have a little reddish tint. Just enough to make me pretty. Occasionally, there is a little tuft of white on our chests. Not mine, but I think my Uncle Decoy has some.

My parents are *"retired"* and older, and they're home most of the time during the day. This is best for my AWS breed. I require daily exercises (*couple of walks would be fine*), but my parents don't walk as good as I do so they have me walk and run beside them in their golf cart. That's a real gas. It's fun and I think I'll say more in another chapter.

Chapter 2

Born *(Eye-Opener)*

The world's lucky day was when I was born on July 22, 2022, in a *"just right sized town"* called *"Beavercreek"*, located in what I was told by my dog parents (*Mom – Piper, Dad – Boomer*), to be a cold wet rainy part of the country. It's a suburb of Portland, Oregon, but I don't know what a suburb is. My dog mother told me I will be getting new human pets (*a mom and a dad*) and I will leave this place. I most likely will travel through Portland to go wherever my new kennel will be. But that day is long away. They also told me that I could be adopted by someone in the Beavercreek area and I would like that because I'm told when it snows, it's a lot of fun to play in. I don't know what snow is but sounds like I might like it.

As I started growing, I thought about the place where I might end but as of this writing, I can't see anything, and I don't know much more than my kennel in Beavercreek, so I go with the flow. I went to Arizona and look what I get to do. Snow. Boy was it fun, just as my dog parents said.

Can't wait until I can see, (*or if I ever will*), so I can see how many siblings I have. Right now, there are too many to count (*I don't know how to count yet*), and I have a lot of those annoying brothers and sisters around me. They are constantly in my way. At this point in my young life, all I do is crawl and roll around and I don't know where I'm going. I just go. So, I bump into my siblings and they are grouches and even try to mouth me. I also sleep a lot and that helps me grow. So far, all I do is **"Drink my moo, do my poo, that's all I do."** I sure hope this life gets better.

Well, I got my wish, my eyes opened, and I can see. That was a long 10 days, especially when you don't have any concept of what 10 days is. The seeing thing is still a little blurry and I don't detect distances particularly good. My color orientation sucks. I'm told I don't see the same colors as my human parents do. The colors I do see are special to dogs. Now that I can see, things like shadows scare me, and bright lights give me the urge to squeal and something is trying to come out, like a bark. At this point it seems more like it's a "yark" instead of a "bark". My squeal is mixed in with it. If you look closely you will notice my eyes are blue. During time, they will change to a brown and yellow/brown. I liked the color of my blue eyes better.

And yes, I've started this thing called walking. I still wobble and it's hard to get my bearings and I don't have much coordination. I just don't know why growing up has to be so hard. My breeder puts us all together in a kennel inside their larger kennel they live in. We could see outside if our kennel were outside. But being inside, I don't get to see outside except when the breeder takes us out for fresh air. It's a big world out there.

All we do in this puppy part of my life is roll around, eat, crawl, eat, whine, eat, sleep, eat, nudge my siblings, eat, and potty wherever I am. We also get some toys to play with and I do like toys. You get the picture......I really like to eat and as I get older, I think I'm still going to like to eat.

I find it's hard enough finding a seat at the dinner table when my siblings are all trying for a seat, and sometimes it's the same seat I'm trying for. I've also found that If you don't answer the dinner bell when it rings, you could miss out. And I like dinner.

My siblings and I have been having a conversation with my dog father *"Boomer"* about how many dog breeds there are, but I don't comprehend much about that now. He keeps saying things like *"There are big dogs"* (*like St Bernard's and Great Danes*), and little dogs like (*Mexican Chihuahuas*) and everything and every color in between. Dad said we all came from a breed called *"wolves,"* back in history. I don't know what wolves are and I don't know anything about history. My life is so short right now, I don't know much of anything. Oh well, as I say, *"it will get better."* I think a good thing about different dog breeds is that our dog language is all the same, no matter which kind of dog you are. My new human parents had conversations about the same thing, and they said different humans from different parts of the country might speak different languages. I'll never know how they can function that way, it must be a mess.

I'm told by my dog parents that this will be the best part of my life. I won't have any responsibilities and all I'll be doing for the next several weeks is eat, sleep, rough house with my siblings, and just have fun. My cup of tea. My dog mom and dad are trying to prepare me for my future. They say we will be going to a new kennel when older and we will enjoy that part of our lives also. We're going to have to go to school at our new kennels, but they will make it fun for us to learn what we are going to have to do in that kennel.

My dog parents are conformation show dogs as well as hunting trial show dogs. My ancestry goes back about 5 generations on a *"pedigree listing"* and most of my relatives are champions in both hunting and confirmation. I guess that means we are some kind of a *"special"* hunting dog. We are very inquisitive and always wondering what a certain *"smell is"* and explore those things we don't understand. That should be fun. My uncle *"Decoy"* went to the Westminster Dog Show a couple of years ago and I think that must have been important. I don't know what I think about that yet. He also participates in barn exercises and runs after some rag or toy. I don't know what I'll have to do when I get older, but everything sounds exciting.

Chapter 3

Education Starts (Airplane & My New Pets)

It's hard to remember my first visit to the Vet. You know, those shots, things stuck up places you don't want them, and the manhandle we go through when the Vet checks us. Judging from where I am now, I must not have liked vets at my first visit, and that could be why I haven't liked them from that time on. But it's a necessary evil.

I had my first airplane ride going to my new pets (*called ParEnTS*) kennel where they live. You notice the word parents has all the letters the word pets has. So, I think the word for my new "pets" is "*parents*". I will go back and forth with those words in this book, because I am still learning about remembering things and I might just forget which one I was using.

One of my breeders flew with me on the airplane from Beavercreek, Oregon, to Tucson, Arizona, so I didn't have to be put with all that baggage. On the airplane, I had to be nice and quiet and stay in a small carrying case my breeder had. It had to be small enough to slide under the seat in front of her. The picture on the left shows you how small it was. I'm not big yet and I barely fit. It was nice because my breeder could carry me in that carrying case. We did drive through Portland, but I didn't get to see much. Just some blue skies outside the windows. The airplane *(this was new to me)* flew from *"Portland"* to a town called *"Seattle"* and after a long wait, we flew on a different airplane to my new hometown called *"Tucson,"* and ended in a suburb *(there's that suburb again)* called *"SaddleBrooke"*. My dog mom was right, this world is bigger than the Kennel I started out in. What a revelation. Almost wish I hadn't been able to see because this big world frightens me.

When I got off the airplane, I was taken outside, and this white vehicle came up where I was waiting, and a couple got out and took me out of my little crate. I was told this was my new parents and I was going to be living in their kennel. My new mom held me in her lap all the way to their kennel in the community called *"SaddleBrooke"*. All these different towns are called *"suburb's"* and that's getting pretty confusing to me. They also call it an active over 55 community. I don't know what an *"over 55 community"* is, but I found out this is a place with lots of *"old people"*. A lot of them have the same problems I had when I came into this world, can't see, walk, hear, and wobble around. They all go to their vets a lot and have someone stick them and shove articles in places they don't like. I haven't seen any crawl around on their bellies like I did, but then I don't see everyone.

My dad made a book before I came to live with them because he wanted to make sure they were aware of all they had to get done before I arrived and even after. You can't read the small print, but you can tell they listed a lot of things they had to do; i.e., get me a kennel, food, toys, vet appointments, pedigree papers, blankets, and just a whole bunch of other stuff. One important thing was the food I had been eating. Dad made sure he got the same food my breeder was feeding me and that was cool. It was fun seeing this when I got to their home but, there are some things on this list that I didn't like; shots, riding in the automobile, and a vet or two that I didn't much care for. But this was what they did to prepare for me.

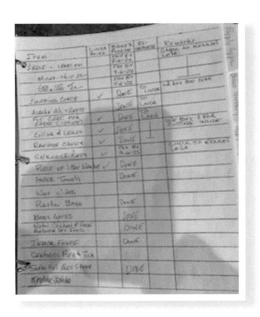

When I got to my parent's kennel, I first noticed a difference in their yard. No grass. All I saw was rocks and I guess that's where I'm supposed to walk and go potty. My feet are a little tender and I'm going to have to get used to those rocks. This is going to be a different world than the one I came from.

Know what, as much as I got irritated with my brothers and sisters' I miss them. All I'm going to have is my parents and their friends, and their friends' pets. I hope all my new friends and parents are as much fun to play with as my siblings. I think it's going to be fun being here, but I'm going to have a lot of work training my new parents to do the things I want them to do.

My first night, I found out I'm going to be sleeping in a kennel by myself and I've never done that before. My kennel is in the same part of their kennel called a *"bedroom."* They have a nice, padded place to lie on in their bedroom, but mine is also pretty nice. They restrict me to my kennel, and I can't go outside by myself yet. They said there are a lot of animals that roam around at night who just might do harm to me. I'm too little to defend myself. So, I'm going to be quiet at night rather than whine and whimper. I didn't do that where I was born, and I'm not going to start now. I hope they like that.

It's funny, but when my parents wake up, they come over to my kennel, pick me up, and hurry to take me outside for my *"potty break."* The ride to get from their bedroom to the outside is fun and I wouldn't want to do anything that would stop that. I don't think they will be able to do that for long, as I will get bigger and I'm sure they won't be able to carry me like they do now. My dog parents, Piper and Boomer, each weighed around 40 pounds and I assume I will weigh the same weight as I get older.

When I was at my kennel with my brothers and sisters, we were trained to do our little duties on something called Astroturf. My new parents don't like that and are trying to train me to go outside on those sharp rocks. I try to go as soon as possible so I don't have to spend much time on those rocks. You know, tender feet. I'll get there someday. I don't understand why they don't want me to go on the Astroturf, so for a while, I'll go on both the Astroturf and the rocks. Maybe I'll win.

I don't have to wiggle and fight for my seat at the dinner table anymore. I'm the only one there. I seem to be able to eat as fast as I want. No one tries to horn in, and I don't have any competition. I think I must have been eating too fast as my parents started feeding me in something with a lot of little places where I have to hunt for my food. It must be a game to my parents, but It now takes me a lot longer to eat and I don't like it much. I was burping a lot before, and this has stopped that. My parents might be a lot smarter than I give them credit for.

My parents have a lot of toys for me to play with, and I really like playing with toys. All the toys are mine and I don't have to share them with another pet. I can chew them, toss them, chase

them, and I've started something on my blankie my parents call *"kneading."* They tell me that a different pet called *"cats"* do this, and I remember doing this when I was younger, sitting at my dinner table. It makes me feel good and I get to think back to when I was with my dog mom *"Piper."* My parents will just have to get used to it, because it makes me feel so good that I don't think I'll quit. I might outgrow it someday, but for now I like it.

My breeder brought some of my toys from my home in Beavercreek, Oregon, and I'm glad she did because it makes me think about being with my brothers and sisters. I thought they were a nuisance when we were all together, but as I said earlier, I miss them now. I'll have to work on my dad and mom being part of my pack and I'm so stubborn I just might become the leader of this pack. This picture is one of the toy's my breeder brought on the airplane, and I still have it today. I really like it and I don't want to tear it up like I've done to some of my toys. I also have a *"Baby Mother"* stuffed toy that has a *"heartbeat"* and I keep this toy in my kennel to sleep with at night. It's really comforting for me and helps me get through the dark nights.

I have lots of other toys, but my favorite toy is still the little pink something or other. I don't know what it's supposed to be, but I played with it after I was born and I must have liked it. I really do like all my toys and by the way, my new parents bought me a lot of toys and I even have some favorites with the new toys. Guess I'm

pretty lucky to have all those toys. I enjoy going to my toy box and picking which toy I want. Naturally, I have to take them all out to see which one I want.

My parents have toys they throw and I chase them and bring them back to where they are. They make me give it to them and toss it again and I have to do this *"retrieve"* thing again and again. Oh well, it's fun and I like running after the toy. I am having fun learning new things, as my parents give me treats when I do it the way they want. As I told you earlier I really do like to eat. I let them *"think"* they're training me, but I'm really training them. I need to get them where I want them to be and that way, I'll have more fun.

I do like my kennel in my parents' bedroom. It's a safe place for me to go when I feel the need. Right now, there are a lot of things that scare me, and the kennel helps me get used to these things. While playing with my toys in the room where my parents watch a *"picture on the wall that moves"* in the evening, I got an idea and took everything out of an area in a small table and started using it as my kennel in this room. It has been a lot of fun and feels just like my kennel in my parent,s kennel bedroom. But I can come and go easier than the kennel in the bedroom.

I wanted to show you the little *"top knot"* I have on the top of my head. Here I'm about 12 weeks old and if you look closely, you'll notice a little "Mohican top knot" on my head. I don't know what a "*Mohican*" is, but I heard my dad and mom call it that. I don't know if I'll outgrow it, but I've seen pictures of others who are older than me that don't have these "*top knots*" anymore. My new mom says she'd like me to keep it because she thinks it's "*adorable*". Everyone that sees me wants to pull my top knot and they say, "*it's cute*".

I'm friendly towards people, too friendly with my parents' weekly dinner guests who come over on Sundays. I just love to jump on these people and it's been hard to ignore me. It's taking a long time to train me not to jump when they arrive, but I'm really training them to let me jump. I do like jumping because they don't stop me and this is the reason I'm training them and not the other way around. My dad keeps telling them how to break me from doing it, but they don't listen. One lady has my number. She immediately barks commands like "*down*", "*sit*", "*stay*", and "*go to your place*". Then she makes me sit and stay in my place until I do calm down. I try to ignore her and when she's on me to do these commands, I try to oblige quickly so she will leave and I can work on the others. She's just not as much fun as the others who let me jump, lick, and mouth them. They just keep giving me rubs, kisses, and tell me how pretty I am. It's hard for me to wait from week to week to see these friends. I seem to have their schedules down and from about 11:00am on Sunday morning, I have to keep watching for these friends to come to dinner.

While I'm friendly towards people, I'm also timid until I get to know them. But once I know them, watch out. I can terrorize anyone by jumping, tail wagging, whining, bark "*hello's*", licking, and just be a nuisance type of greeting.

I don't want you to think that all the work is on my parents' side of the equation, because I had a lot to learn and it takes time to learn some of those commands. I'm little and just learning those basic commands. But between us, we have all managed to make the best of both our situations and I don't think either of us would change anything or would even want to.

It was nice coming into their home kennel and I hope you enjoy this writing about my *1st year with the Baker's; Bampa and Grandma Darbie* as much as I did living it.

Chapter 4

Learning (New Kennel & Toys)

When I got to my new parent's kennel, they wanted me to sleep in a kennel that's my size in their "*bedroom*". I guess it's ok because I feel safe when I'm in there. Like I said earlier, I still miss my brothers and sisters, so I think I need the safety of the kennel. I'm going to be quiet during the night in my new kennel as thanks to my new parents for getting it for me. I think I already told you my breeder sent a stuffed toy "*mommy*" that has a heartbeat, and this is in my new kennel for me to sleep with at night. I like it.

My parents said they have never had a dog trained to a kennel before and this was going to be a first. My new dad trained me to the kennel, and I surprised him by learning it as early as I did. It took him less than a couple of times to get me to run down the hall when he said, **"kennel up"**. My parents liked seeing me hop and run, and my ears flopping "*to-and-fro*". Dad also trained me to sit, stay, down, place, and ok. He did this early on, but when I became around 4-5 months old, he decided I needed more commands to work on. I have one thing I still have trouble with. I really like my parents and their friends so much that I jump on them and wag my tail (*I finally found out why I have it*). I guess it's a nuisance because dad is always saying "*off*". I like seeing everyone so much it's hard to quit.

Since my parents are older, they felt they should teach me to be more courteous than I thought I should. I don't mind it and I learned some of these things early on. They want me to wait for them to go through a door first and then I go. I'm supposed to walk beside them at the same pace they do and when they stop, I'm supposed to sit beside them. I was used to going after my food in a disorderly manner and rushing the food dish, but my parents want me to wait until they say "ok". Guess it works for them, but it now takes me a little longer for me to start eating. Maybe I'll get there, but for now, my parents hold up my dish until I do what they want. And it's easier for me to just do it because I found out I get to eat quicker if I do. I'm really training them to have my food ready at the same time every day. This other stuff I have to go through is just something I have to put up with to get them to do what I want them to do.

I wrote about our Sunday's because my parents have friends over for dinner and they talk and tell jokes and play games. I guess they like getting together and they all have some fun. It's fun being petted by everyone and running from person to person. Now that I'm older, I get to lay at their feet when they're playing games at the table. I also get to lay around or play with those who are not playing a game. As I get older, I don't have as many "she's cute" comments like I used to. But I know they really like me because some try to feed and pet me.

Dad hired a lady trainer, and she started out very quickly with some of the same basics my dad did. Dad had me trained to sleep in my new kennel ever since the first night. Like dad said earlier, I never whimper at night, and there hasn't been any sleep loss because I was in my new kennel. Dad says whatever the breeder did was "right on" because I'm well suited for this life. I've been trained "NOT" to go through the door before my parents, and to "sit and stay" before I start eating. Dad said this was because they're older, and they didn't want me running to get where we all were going and making my parents "slip and fall". However, I learned all these new tricks and my parents say I'm a joy to them and they enjoy every minute I'm with them. I know, I've said this before, but there has to be some duplications in these chapters. Hooray, I'm a pleasure to be around and my plan is working.

I weighed 9 pounds when my new parents got me. I'm growing pretty fast, but my parents say I'm only growing "half-fast". I don't know what that means, but they laugh when they say it. My parents like the way I hop around. I don't know why I do it, but they laugh and think it's cute, so I'll continue.

I also had to learn to go to the potty outside. When I was with my brothers and sisters, my mom (*Piper*), would keep us clean and there wasn't too much of a mess. Getting older, my breeder wanted us to go on something called Astro Turf. I just got used to that and now my new mom and dad want me to go outside.

I learned something that I guess is funny to my new parents and their friends. I was sitting on my dad's lap and a commercial came on the TV about *"Liberty Auto Insurance"*. The commercial had three (3) people sitting at a table in a pie eating contest. The table was on a Pier and while on the Pier, some big birds started flying in just before those people started eating the pies. When the birds did that, I started barking at the birds. Don't know why I had the urge to do that, but now every time I see that commercial on TV, I start barking. My parents and their friends enjoy seeing me do this. Dad says he'd like to teach me to bark at a political party when they come on the TV, but he hasn't done that. Oh well, another treat...

I require daily exercises (couple of walks would be fine), but my parents don't walk as good as I do so they have me walk and run beside them in their golf cart. **I** really like this as I'm a muscular breed and have lots of stamina. When we head for the garage, dad commands me to sit and stay while he puts my special leash on me. He goes through the door first and then commands me to *"heal"* and we head towards the golf cart. He gives me a command "slowly" to get me to slow down when walking beside him. He then commands me to *"load up"* and I run and jump inside and sit on the seat and we both wait for mom. He then pushes this button thingy and the garage door starts going up and then we back out. When mom gets in, we drive to the end of the driveway and dad says *"heal"*. This gets me started and the first thing I do is jump out of the golf cart and run as fast as I can up the road in front of my parent's kennel to the corner. I really like to run fast. My ears flop and my running is more of a hop than a run. All I know is that dad has to make his golf cart go fast to keep up with me. I just love the breeze going through my hair and this invigorates me. When we come to the stop sign, dad says *"stop"*, then *"sit"*, and we all look both ways for automobiles or people. He then says *"heal"* again and starts left and again, I want to run as fast as I can. This goes on for maybe a half block then I decide to slow down to a trot and later a fast walk. We go for 3 miles on one route and 3.5 miles on the other route, and this is what I call *"fun"*. While smells inside the home are good, you know, food and all, the outside has so many smells and I have so much fun trying to tell them apart. I have met other dogs around here and I smell them when I'm on my morning exercise *walk and run*. But there are a lot of other smells I'm not familiar with and I don't know if I would like them or not. But to a hunting dog, this smell outside is just the best. When I get home, I head to my water dish (*dad puts ice in it*) and water tastes so good when you've exercised. I look forward to this every morning. Don't tell my parents, but it's almost as good as eating food.

I recently learned a couple of new things. We went on a *"vacation"*, I didn't know what a vacation was, but do now. I had to learn *"load up"* to get into their automobile. I had to learn that a car was a fun way to ride. First day was miserable. Second day wasn't much better, but eventually it got better. When we arrived at my dad's cousin's house, in Wichita Kansas, I found out we were going to stay with him, and he has a gazillion stairs in his house. I like that word "gazillion". It's big for me.

Yep, I had to learn how to go up and down stairs. The going down scared me more than going up, but I didn't like it either way and it took me a couple of days to learn. After I got the hang of it, I liked running up and down the stairs. It's fun. More in Chapter 9.

I also had to learn how to get along with the neighbor's dogs. They lived on both sides. One side had a Rottweiler/Blood Hound mix, and the other side had two large Eskimo Huskies. Dad says that dogs don't know their own size, but I'm telling you, I knew those dogs were a lot bigger than me. And to tell the truth, when riding in the car, I see all kinds of dogs. Big ones, small ones, and all colors. Just like my dad "Boomer" said.

It seems like I have to learn something new every day. I guess that's part of growing up and someday I'll know everything. But my world is getting easier as I grow more and I've figured out that the older I get, the more I'll know. Sounds neat.

The neat thing about my parents' kennel is that it's big. It seems like that to me, but I'm little and everything seems big. They have a lot of smaller kennels inside their big one. When I first came to my parent's kennel, they restricted me to only a few smaller kennels. They had some kind of a door or gate thing that was my cue telling me I can't go in there. Even at one year old, I'm still restricted when they want.

When I first arrived at my parent's kennel, I had my own little kennel in the kennel called *"the family room"*. They also had a small fence that I didn't like very much. So, I immediately went to work pushing my blankets into the corner and then I could climb up and at that point I could jump (*or rather fall*) out. That didn't last long and a couple of days later, I saw that stupid fence on the back patio. I never went into that again. Training my parents is not so hard, they learn fast.

My parents go potty inside their *"potty kennel"*. Wish they had to walk outside like I do and go over those sharp little rocks. I bet they would change that quickly. They have a kennel for their car and another bedroom kennel as well as an office and utility room kennel. Lot of kennels in this place.

We also have a kitchen kennel and a breakfast kennel in the same room (*family room kennel*) where they want me during the day. I also have a bed inside my very own kennel in the bedroom kennel. They have it padded nicely and it's pretty neat to have my own sleeping kennel.

Little do they know I'm training them to let me get on the furniture, They are not allowing me on the furniture and it looks so comfy. I can't jump up there now because of my size but in the future you better watch out, because I'm going to train them to let me get on one part of the couch. I'm sure I can get them to put a pad on that sofa chair and that should be comfy. **Note: Update,** I finally trained my parents to let me have one chair I can call my own. It took a while, but I finally won out and trained them to put pads down and let me use it whenever I want. Hooray.....

I've learned that this world is *"give and take"*. I'm wondering if that means my parents need to be trained to give and I'm already trained to take. That should make for a fun time for all.

I think enough said about *"kennels"*. The real goal here is to train my parents to be good at what they learn. It'll be good for all of us.

Chapter 5

Place (My "Place" in My New Pets Home)

I know you are going to read into this that my parent's kennel is my place. While it is, the *"my place"* I really like is in the family room. They bought a pet trampoline and it was way bigger than I, but I'm sure I'll grow into it. They also put a blanket on the trampoline and that makes it nice and comfy. I love to run towards the trampoline and dive through the air and land in the middle. It's fun but makes a lot of commotion.

This is a picture (*I'm a little older in the picture*) of my *"Place"* in the family room. My parents tell me to go there whenever they want me to. Sometimes when I don't mind they send me to my *"place"* and tell me to *"sit"* and *"stay"*. I also play with my toys pretty much all the time and I usually have them around my *"place"* most of the time. They don't understand that I like my toys so much it's easier for me to have them close to me.

My parents have started telling me to *"go to my place"* and pointing to other areas where they want me to be. I was in The Home Depot and we were walking down the aisle and they sent me to a "place", and it turned out to be where floor mats were. My dad just pointed to where he wanted me, and I went. I guess that pleased him. I think the message is that any place they point to is going to be my *"place"* if they want it to be. Guess I'm lucky because I have *lots of places*.

I really like being around my parents, but it does cause some situations that aren't easy to cope with. Even though I'm timid around new humans I don't know, I am very nice around those I know. As I said earlier, my parents have a dinner every Sunday and I know everyone in the group. I only see them a week and I really want to greet them, but my method of greeting is different that humans. I jump, lick, and smell in places that aren't comfortable for humans. I get so excited that sometimes I pee a bit and that makes for a bad entrance between me and those who just came in. Usually, a bunch comes at once and I jump around and go from person to person. If they would only ignore me I would calm down and just walk around. It is always a problem when these humans show up. This is when my parents send me to my *"place"*, and I have to *"sit"* there for a long

period of time until I calm down. Then they let me go to the friends and I get to say *"hi"*. My parents hope I outgrow this, but I don't know.....

I also have lots of places in stores when I get to go there with my parents. Sometimes they want to look at something and they send me to something out of the way and tell me to *"place"* and *"stay"*. So far, I think it's a good thing and I enjoy the loving, petting, nice words that come with my actions.

As I said earlier, Dad and Mom took me to Home Depot, which is a big, huge store where they have all kinds of stuff and I could go wild in there if I had the chance. The smells are different and that pleases me. Anyway, they walk me up and down the aisles, have me sit and stay, and even commanded me to *"place"* in odd places. They say place, sit and stay and just walk away. There were a lot of people who came by and saw me and I just sat there and waited for dad and mom to give the command *"come"*.

I am also close to my parents and that is what I want more than anything. So, I have a lot of *"places"* in a store. One day in my back yard, my parents told me to sit on a rock. I did it, but I really didn't care for it much. Sometimes, I'm afraid my parents are going to get used to this *"place"* thing, and I don't see an end to it. Oh, well, I may have to put up with it.

Chapter 6

Meeting Dogs (Others Have Pets Like Mine)

After I was born, the only other dogs I knew were my mom and dad (*Piper & Boomer*), some aunts and uncles, and 5 siblings. I didn't even know if they were boys or girls. My world was small, but I didn't know it at the time. After my airplane ride to my new parent's kennel, I was not allowed to meet any dogs because I hadn't had all of my puppy shots. I didn't know this puppy part of my life was going to be hard to accept, but that chapter is coming up. I'm not so sure I want to grow up and leave the puppy part. For the most part, it's fun.

After I got through that awful *"getting puppy shots"* period of my life, I met dogs on the road when mom took me for a walk. We run into people who have dogs, and I must admit that some of them don't mind very well. My mom makes me sit at her side when we meet someone else, even if they don't have dogs. But that's ok because I'm still a little scared when it comes to meeting others.

Occasionally mom and I walked with dad's cousin, who lives down the street from us. She has a lot of dogs, and most of them are big, even though dad says dogs don't know their size. I believe they have one St. Bernard and four Afghans, and one itty bitty poo of some kind. I had a lot of fun with those dogs when they came over to my back yard, but it appears to me I must have become somewhat of a nuisance. I ran around them in my back yard, and we all seemed to enjoy it. But, one day I went to a friend of moms who had a small dog (*like me*). My dad's cousin was also there with her pack, and I was excited to see them. I ran to everyone getting ready to play tag and all of a sudden, they started coming after me like I had done something wrong. I turned and bolted and ran back to mom and got between her legs. I wanted to say *"help me"* but all I can do is bark, and I did a lot of that.

When we went on our vacation to Kansas and Oklahoma, I met some new dogs. My dad's cousin lives in Wichita Kansas, and (*I didn't know it at the time*), he has big dogs on both sides of him. And I mean BIG dogs. On one side was a Rottweiler, and on the other side two Alaskan Huskies. Now those are BIG dogs. Well, I was just feeling comfortable in the house with all those stairs, and I went outside to take a potty break. The house has a *"sun deck"* on the back and since it's a split-level home, there's stairs down the back of his sun deck to the back yard. So, this day I casually walked onto the sun deck, and it was neat because I could look around the neighborhood and see so much. Also, a lot of smells that I enjoyed. I headed down the nine (9) stairs and explored the fenced back yard when all of a sudden I heard a loud *"Ruff"* in a deep voice. I turned and looked towards the direction of the *"ruff"* and saw one of the largest dogs I've seen in quite a while. It was a *"Rottweiler"/"Hound Dog"* mix. Scared me to death and I quickly turned and ran as fast as my little legs would carry me back up those stairs to the *"sun deck"* where mom was. I got between her legs and poked my head out and looked at that big dog. Boy did that scare me.

I met the two Alaskan Huskies on the other side much the same way, except they tried to dig under the fence to get to me and that scared me. Again, mom to the rescue. Making a long story short, I got to know these dogs and by the second day we were running up and down the back yard fences and enjoying it. Maybe dad was right, dogs don't know size.

On another note, my dad's sister has a **"Brittney Spaniel, named Brandy"**, who is kind of protective of her home. We were all going there to visit, but they ended up leaving me at the cousin's home with him dog sitting. Dads' sister thought "*Brandy*" would be mad at me and beat me up. Can you imagine how I felt being left at my age. After all, I was 10 months old by then. But I was glad I didn't go because I don't like confrontations and now that I know the reason, I would have been a scared. This is not a picture of Brandy, but dad didn't have one so we just used a picture dad had. They are cute dogs though and Brandy is a good dog, even though I would have been scared. After all, I'm still a puppy at heart.

Guess we might never know if she would have been mad enough to snap at me. I'm sure I'll meet her when I get older.

The community where I live has a dog park and I've been there once. There are people who think dog parks are fun and good for socialization, whatever that means. Some think there might be too many different diseases at these dog parks. Dad likes to go there, and I think it's because he gets some socialization. Like I said, I've only been there once. I don't think our breeder was too keen on dog parks as well as my new vet.

Chapter 7

Automobile *(First Ride)*

My second (2) and third (3) automobile rides in Tucson were disasters. My first being from the airport to my new parent's kennel and I was held all the way. That's the good way to ride in an automobile. My next two rides were within a few days after I got to my new parent's home. I was only 9 ½ weeks old and my rides were to a veterinarian for something sharp that my parents called a *"shot"*. Dad had a kennel in the back of his automobile similar to the one in the bedroom, and I was just getting used to my kennel and all of a sudden, they took me to this big monster thing that has wheels and put me in the back in that kennel. This also confused me as the only kennel I'd been in for traveling was a small carrying kennel lying on the floor in an *"airplane"*. It was a long time before we got there, and I sure let my parents know I wasn't happy. I whined and cried all the way and even got sick in the car and threw up. That didn't feel good. I don't remember having that feeling before. Mom and Dad had a mess to clean up. This trip to the Vet was not a winning situation for anyone, and for me it was a losing situation.

Guess what, I did the same thing going home. Whined, cried, was really anxious, slobbered, and had *"hang daddy's"*, as my dad calls them. He told mom that hang daddies were drooling from my mouth and were running down my chest and everything in the vicinity was wet. I was drenched when we got home. They said they were going to work on riding in an automobile. My parents told someone I must be part *"cat"* because they called me a *"scaredy cat"*. I still don't know what a *"cat"* is, but the comment didn't make me feel good.

I'm going to have to get used to it, because it seems everywhere we go is so far that we have to get in that big thing on wheels called an *"automobile"*. I've hated it every time. I really didn't get much time to get used to the automobile before our *"vacation"*. My dad even tricked me into getting into the automobile and I'm not too happy about that.

Before we left on our vacation trip, he taught me to *"load up"* and jump into the back seat of this automobile. I really had a good seat, because dad put some covers all around and it was like a cave with no top. There were even compartments for my toys. Well.... Dad shut the door and that was it. Always before Dad opened the door and I got out. Not this time, I was in *"jail"*. More about this in Chapter 9.

Chapter 8

Veterinarian *(Meeting My Vet)*

My first vet was a lady vet, substituting for the owner. I really liked her, and she was nice to me. She talked to me when she felt certain areas of my body and gave me treats in the process. The shot didn't even bother me. I really liked the first vet I saw and enjoyed the visit. I have now changed my mind about vets, because my first visit as a puppy must have scared me and I thought all vets were mean. This vet was pretty cool and giving me treats whenever she handled me was pretty nice. Yes. She was cool.

My second vet was also a lady, but not so cool. I didn't meet her when I first went to the vet. She was the owner and the first lady vet was the one filling in for her. I was looking forward to meeting her when I went to my appointment. After a short while of examining me, she shoved something in the other end of my body and that was unexpected, and I yelped (*a new sound for me*) and got out of her hands and ran to mom and tried to hide under her chair. That was an experience I didn't want again. The other person in the room with this vet was called a "*vet tech*", and she was kind. She caught me and held me in her lap and gave me a treat and I calmed down. My dad asked the vet to clip my nails. I didn't know what to expect and the vet grabbed me and held me while she took this tool and put it on one of my front paws nails and squeezed the tool. That was a new feeling for me, and I hadn't had it before. I don't think it hurt, but it really felt weird, and I didn't like it. Again, I yelped, and the vet told dad she was going to have to take me into the back room to clip my nails. Dad said, *"don't bother, we'll do it at home"*. Boy was I glad he said that. That was the end of my appointment, and I was ready to get *"out of Dodge"*. By the way, my parents both cut my nails and they use a Dremel. I also get treats during the process and you know I like treats.

Later, I got my first UTI (*urinary tract infection*) and dad and mom had to take me to the vet to find out how to treat my problem. Well, dad called the vet I had been going to for my puppy shots (*the one I didn't like*) and tried to get me in for an appointment. No luck, they said they didn't have any slots to fit me in. Not being able to get me into our vet upset dad and he started calling other vets. He even called the vet where the substitute worked full time when she wasn't filling in for someone and they said they didn't have any times they could see me. Dad said, *"you have 6 vets and no slots for emergencies"*? The lady said *"no"*. Dad told the lady that *"I had seen one of their vet's and could we get an appointment to see her"*. The lady said *"no"*, we don't have anything. Then dad got mad and asked the lady **"Does your clinic even like animals"**? He was really upset with that receptionist.

After many phone calls, dad finally got the name of a *"Traveling (Mobile) Vet"*, and he agreed to come to our home that afternoon. He was nice. Brought his scale in to weigh me (*I weighed about 37 pounds*) and he gave me an exam. He gave me a shot and some pills and told my dad I would get better. He also had a nice Vet truck with a neat laboratory inside with lots of equipment. I could have had a lot of fun if I was left alone in there. I could make a mess. Dad was impressed with him and it was a good visit. Dad then ask if he was taking new clients and the answer was yes. So, dad immediately signed us up and he's even had to come out again. He's nice.

Dad bought me a dog (*pet*) scale and even taught me to *"sit and stay"* and not move to disrupt the scale. I have to sit quietly and when the numbers slow to a stop, I'm supposed to *"not move"*. He then gives me a treat after he reads the weight. It's fun. I now weigh 43.2 pounds. I'm a little big right now and my parents have me on a diet. I don't like that diet much and I complain all the time, but for some reason I don't win. If dad would only weigh me every day, I would get a lot of treats, but that might not help my weight loss.

I also started my "heat" cycle when I was only 8 months old and that was a real bummer. I didn't know what the heck that was, and I don't think my parents knew what to do. Anyway, I had to wear a diaper every day for about 3 weeks and that was a real pain in the you-know-what. I guess they didn't want me making messes in the house and I know they didn't want me to have any boyfriends. I found out that a "heat cycle" is the time that I could start the process to have puppies. I'm glad my parents were there to help. I'm also not going to ever have any puppies because my parents told me I'm going to be "spayed". Wow, that must have been a big deal. I don't know if I would have wanted any puppies either. I remember my dog mom "Piper", and how tired she was most of the time.

I also came down with another UTI during my heat cycle. I'm getting tired of this, and I'm told this spaying thing can correct some of that. It's definitely no fun and it hurts. But my parents are there to help and that makes me feel better. I don't know what I'd do without them. They have been comforting.

I heard dad and mom talking and they were addressing the "spaying" thing. They both were commenting that I had beautiful confirmation, and they were sorry I'm not going to get to compete. They said, "if we were younger, it would have been a lot of fun to show me". What does that have to do with spaying? I guess I would have to be able to have puppies if I was to become a show dog. My parents said they're too old for that, and they didn't want to send me to someone else to have my puppies, so just prior to my first birthday, I got spayed. Dad said maybe I could go to some other kind of shows, like obstacle course racing, some barn thingy, and some endurance races. I'm really strong and I can run fast. I also have a good sense of smell when it comes to birds and things when we walk and run on the golf course in the evening. I can't get those smells out of my system, but I have fun wanting to run after anything I see and smell. Wish dad could shoot a bird, so I could retrieve it. Maybe there are some other things I can do.

I look on *"Brags and Wags"*, on Facebook and see other AWS dogs and I know it would be fun to do what some of them do. I also have a distant cousin living in Arkansas who is a good hunter. I haven't met him yet but will someday. His name is *"Red"* and he's lucky. He lives on 40 acres and has the run of the place. That would be fun.

Chapter 9

Vacation (First One)

My parents decided to take a trip and called it a "vacation". I didn't know what a vacation is, but I heard them talking about it. I think I'm going because I heard them talking about including me. I heard things like *"boarding"*, *"neighbor offered"*, *"Day Care"*, and *"riding in the car"*. If that is a *"vacation"*, there might be something fun involved. The *"fun"* part of the vacation trip sounds *"exciting"*. I always like things to do.

My parents said they needed to go to dad's high school reunion in Salina, Kansas and he had to go see his sister and cousin in Wichita, Kansas. He also wanted to see his best friend in Ada, Oklahoma and combine all this in the trip. It sounds like a lot of going and doing. As I said earlier, I like people and love jumping up and down around them. And it all sounds fun.

I could tell this was exciting to my parents because they brought some red cases into the house from the garage and put them in the secret bedroom they didn't let me go into. I really want to go into that bedroom, but they always shut the door. A couple times I found the door open, and I did sneak inside that room. I saw lots of things under the bed and on the walls, and everywhere around. But not to be for me. I don't know what makes me want to go into there. Nothing to chew on, or throw around and chase, and no bed to go to sleep on. It is carpeted and I know I could have had a potty accident when I was young, but now I'm potty trained.

Anyway, back to the vacation. They decided that I was going, and I was glad to hear that. They put clothes inside their red bags, then took my kennel *(from dad and moms' bedroom)*, my toys, my food and a lot of stuff I didn't know what it was. When I looked at the number of trips they made to the car, It looked like a lot of stuff is making its way into that car plus dad, mom, and me.

As I said earlier, dad taught me a new command called *"Load Up"*. He would open the door and give the command *"load up"* and I would jump up and into the seat in the car. That seat is *"mine"* and is right behind mom's seat. It's nice having my own seat. In fact, I have all the seat *(they call it a back seat)*, except where some clothes hang on one side but I found I can use them to sleep beside.

Well, this morning, dad wanted to show mom my new trick. So, he told her to go with him and he would show her something new. I healed by his side through the garage and when we got to the car he opened the door. I sat there and dad said, *"load up"* and in I jumped. Dad shut the car door and dad and mom walked away. I thought to myself *"wait a minute"*, *"you forgot me"*. That didn't make any difference to them, and they casually walked around the car, got in and started the car, and backed out. I had never done this part of the trick before and I was starting to get anxious and realized I was the one tricked. Anyway, we started down the highway with my mouth drooling, real nervous, and whimpering.

That car must have driven a couple of years' worth of miles off my age. I didn't much care for it. Dad had toys fixed in the pads he made for the back seat and that was nice, but at the time I didn't like it. Needless to say, we drove all day and I got out a couple of times to do my duty, but I continued to be nervous and I didn't play with any toys. Who could do that under these circumstances.

Before we stopped for the night, we went to a restaurant and dad and mom ordered food to go. We then stopped at something called a motel and they took me inside to a big room. That was our evening. Watching TV, planning the next day, and going to sleep. That was a nice place and I enjoyed being out of that car. The next morning, we did everything all over again.

We started driving I must admit it wasn't as bad as the day before and I was able to concentrate on the outside scenery. Every now and then a "*whoosh*" went past me and scared me. Mom told me it was a truck passing and the noise was only wind, but I didn't expect it to be like it sounded. Guess I am just an ole scaredy cat. I didn't drool and was able to lay down and my anxiousness seemed less. I really did start enjoying it.

I brought up the following in Chapter 4 and the bigger explanation is here. The next day was when we got to Wichita, Kansas and I saw an old friend, my dad's cousin. This was another part of the trip that I wasn't aware I would have to learn something. I now had to learn how to navigate **"STAIRS"**. I had never learned that before because I had never been around stairs. Anyway, to let you know, there's 6 stairs going into the house, 15 stairs down and 15 stairs up from his basement, where I found out that's where we're going to sleep. Since his home is a "split entry", there's 6 stairs going up from the basement into the back yard. There are 9 stairs going up from his back yard to his sun deck, and 6 stairs going into his garage from the kitchen. Stairs, stairs, stairs........ Dad said I looked like a worm slinking up and down the stairs. They laughed, but I didn't find anything funny. I think I learned something about numbers while we stayed with dad's cousin.

After I learned about the stairs, I found I could run up and down. That became a new game for me and one I wanted to play a lot. It was fun. The next trip in the car was from the Cousins house to his high school friend and his wife in Ada Oklahoma. That ride was ok. Not too long, but I still didn't play with my toys, and I got more used to looking out the window, laying down and taking a nap, and I just plain liked it. Hope they take me around more with them after we get home.

They have a big.. big.. yard, lot of land, and they had a lot of grass. It was fun running around their yard as they were in farm country. There were chickens and other dogs in a neighbor's yard and after I got used to them, they were even fun. Dad was a little worried about me and chickens. Maybe because they looked like birds. No problem.

They had two (2) dogs, both "*toy poodle's*". They were older than I, and I must have irritated them as they growled and snapped at me all the time. I kept trying to make friends, but they must have thought I was a nuisance. They couldn't stop me as I'm really quick with my movements and it was fun agitating them and jumping out of range when they snapped. I can make fun out of anything.

The trip home was quite uneventful. By this time, I was a seasoned traveler and I slept a lot of the time. I also spent time looking at the scenery. I did get to sleep in the bed with my parents in the motel and that was probably the coolest part of the trip. I had never done that before and it was their suggestion, so I wasn't going to get into trouble. We were in the dog wing of the motel and my parents thought I was going to bark at the people and dogs going back and forth in the hall. Dad said, "*better have Sadie sleep in our bed, maybe she'll be quiet*". It worked. It was just plain fun. Actually, everything I did on this trip was fun. Someday, maybe I'll get to go again.

Chapter 10

First Bath (Then Another One)

This was not a day for me to start out on new adventures. But evidently mom and dad thought I needed a *B-A-T-H*. Don't they know I'm an American Water Spaniel and I get all the baths I need outdoors.

I didn't even know my parents got a picture of my first bath. It wasn't something I wanted to do, but I'm too little to argue. So, I did the only thing I could do at my age; I made funny sounds, whined, and even learned to bark while in their sink. But I guess it's for my best hygiene and medical fitness and I must admit it feels good. Dad put soap on my back and with his fingers, he rubbed and kind of scratched, and that really felt good.

I heard my parents say something to the order of *"we need to get a water pool for Sadie so she can act like an American Water Spaniel"*. My parents do have a water feature in their back yard, and I can sneak into that if I really want to. So far, I haven't had time to sneak.

As I got older, I progressed to another type of bath. Maybe that's because I am now heavier, and my parents can't pick me up. We now have *"shower time"*, and it's an *"all-together"* shower time. My parents take showers every day, but I only get one on a once-a-week schedule. I don't know schedules yet, so I never know when that once a week is about to happen, then *"Boom they grab me and off to the shower I go"*. Now we all get into the shower and they both *"dog abuse"* me by one parent holding, and the other putting this stuff on me and rubbing me until I'm all soaped up. Then it's time to put some kind of a rinse on me (*they say it helps the soap get off my body*), and then more water to get whatever is still on me off. It actually feels good, but I bet the reason there's no picture of that in this book, is because *"that probably wouldn't be a good picture"*.

The next part I like, they have these great big towels, and they use them to rub me until I start drying. That really feels good and I'm sorry I can't get ahold of those towels and play with them, because I would like to play rough house. I think dragging them around on the floor would be great fun. They keep them hid from me and so far I haven't been able to find them. Anyway, this rubbing feels so good and after my parents are finished, they let me rub my body on those towels by putting them on the floor and saying, *"OK Sadie, go get'em"*. From there I go to our bedroom and get my *"mommy stuffed animal"*, which is the one I brought with me from *Beavercreek Kennels in Oregon*. Mom doesn't want me to tear it up, so she only lets me have her at night when I *"Kennel Up"* to go to sleep. She has a heartbeat inside the toy. Pretty neat. I also rub myself on the rugs on the floor and they feel just as good.

I guess this shower thing is pretty cool. I know I smell better (*I can smell more things than mom and dad*), my hair seems softer, and humans like to pet, rub, and scratch me after I shower. I guess I really like it too. Anyway, I'm going to have to get used to it because I'm sure I'll have to do it for many years. *Whoopee!*

Well, I've grown up to *"almost my adult size"*, and by now I do like showers. I don't know what this AWS name for me means, but I keep hearing my dad say, *"she's definitely not a water dog*", and then he laughs as he's washing me in the shower. I just don't like all that handling, holding, and that awful stuff with bubbles. But I must admit I'm enjoying my showers more. I really like the rubbing and the good feeling I get when they rub their hands all over my body.

Showers are a family thing in this Baker household. Mom and dad get down to their "Au *naturel*" fashion, and of course, I'm always "Au naturel". Then the bubble stuff starts coming on, followed by that great rubbing. I always look forward to the part where they take the handheld object (*where the water comes out*) and get all the bubblies off me. That feels good. The feeling I get when they wash my face is enjoyable. It makes me think of why my registered name is *"Beavercreek Beautiful Princess"*.

Chapter 11

First Christmas (What Fun)

I was born July 22, 2022, so I was only 5 months old when my first Christmas came around. That seemed a long time to me, but in the scheme of things, it was a very short period of my life. It's difficult to think that I would be happy and have a good time doing something that was new to me. Of course, everything is new to me at this stage in my life.

This was a royal pain in the rear. Dad and mom put Pjs on me when I woke up on Christmas morning. I didn't know why they did it, but guess I'll find out later. It seems they're going to celebrate a *holiday* and I don't know what a *"holiday"* is. I soon found out and it's a lot of fun.

My parents had a large Christmas tree in their living room with lots of neat stuff hanging all over and I just knew I could have fun getting my mouth around everything. I mouthed a couple of things on the tree a few times and my dad and mom told me to quit doing that. *I didn't.* It was fun. One time I got a little round man with a white beard in my mouth and when dad said, *"give me that"*, I ran, and he

chased me. That was a new game to me, and it was fun. I'm pretty good on my 4 legs now, and I can run faster than dad. He also has this stick he uses when he walks, and I think that slows him down. Oh well, it is a fun game. When he caught me, he told me to *"release"*, and then he said, *"good girl"*, and that was neat. Dad and mom took everything off the tree after Christmas and it's kind of drab now. Just a plain ole green tree. Maybe they'll decorate it next Christmas. By then, I'll be older and maybe I can figure out how to get some of those hanging down things and enjoy Christmas all over again.

A neighbor left a package at our front door, and it was for me. Of course, this was new to me, and dad and mom told me to *"tear it up"*, and immediately I thought *"this is going to be fun"*. So, I got busy and shook it, pushed it around the room with my nose, growled at it to let it know whose boss, and bit into the box and tore the paper off. Then I had to attack the box after I got the paper off. And I got to do all of this with no one yelling at me except to say, *"go get it girl"*, and *"shake it"* so it made noise. I got to move it around, grab the paper, rip it, and make the biggest mess. I really do like to make messes because it's so much fun. I wish they would let me do it all the time. Well, as luck would have it, I finally got it opened and it was a new chew toy for me and has become one of my favorites. It's a toughie and I can't tear it up, but I really enjoy trying.

I did have fun on Christmas and wished we had Christmas every day. Now I can't wait until next Christmas. I'm sure there'll be another one, and I'm going to be prepared. I have my bigger teeth now and I can really rip into things and make bigger messes. I can also run faster than my dad, so I know I'll have fun.

Christmas was a fun time for me. There were lots of extras for me to play with and get into trouble. A lot of people came over at different times and that's fun. I even snuck some candy a time or two and that tasted like nothing I had eaten before. Sure, gave me energy.

Chapter 12

Trouble (Hey, I'm a Hunting Dog)

I said there are some doors shut to me, a guest bathroom, the office, and a guest bedroom. Well, I found out why. The bathroom has a couple of baskets under the counter and in those baskets are some bathroom towels. When I start looking at them, my parents always tell me to *"leave them alone"*. Now, that's difficult for me because they're baskets and baskets just might be *"fun chewing"*. I think I've been pretty good in the *"not chewing department"*. I've never chewed on furniture (*where there's a lot of wood*), and I've never tried to get on the furniture, so I don't take naps on the furniture. I have my trampoline and a comfy rug on the floor where I take naps during the day.

An update to this *"not getting on the furniture"* activity....I now have one chair I'm allowed on. I try to steal additional space to make my space larger, but I get corrected every time.

Anyway, back to the bathroom. I think *chewing on these baskets would be fun* because they're different. One time the door was open and my dad was working in the office. I snuck into the bathroom, pulled out a basket with those towels, washcloths, and hand towels, and dragged the basket into the hall. Now dad was only about 12 feet away, and I guess he was busy with something and didn't hear or see me. Wow now was my chance. I took the towels and everything else out of the basket. This was starting to be fun. Then I planted my teeth around the top of the basket and sunk them into the webbing. I got to take some bites into basket and little pieces of webbing started to fall on the floor. Suddenly this became more fun.

Well, all good things come to an end. Dad went to the printer to get something, and when he turned around, he yelled at me, "*Sadie, what are you doing*", and I knew right away I was in trouble. He grabbed everything, me included and really scolded me. I went to my place in the family room and didn't get off for quite a while. I knew dad was mad and I don't like him to be mad at me.

Another thing I got into trouble for was *when I took my dad's hearing aid* and decided to carry it around in my mouth for a while. I do that with leaves and things I pick up in the backyard. I don't swallow the leaves, but I swish them around in my mouth so my parents don't know I have something. Well, I didn't swallow the hearing aid, but every now and then I had to position it in my mouth so no one would know. Well, mom caught me doing that and said "*Sadie, take that out of your mouth*", then said "*release*". I did release the main part of the hearing aid, *but bit off the end where the microphone* is and that's the part that

goes into dad's ear. Then I swallowed it. I'm not going to say it tasted good, but I did it only as a reaction to mom. Maybe if I swallow, no one will notice. Guess that strategy didn't seem to work. Anyway, I found out that wasn't the neatest thing to do.

Next day, Mom brought my potties into the house for examination. I thought "*ugh, glad I'm not a mom*". Then, after a while examining my potty, she said "*found it*". Dad called the store and they said if the part behind the ear wasn't damaged, they could fix it, so off he went. I did leave a tooth mark on the hearing aid when mom got onto me. Dad said it cost him $75.00. He decided that because part of his hearing aid went through me, he didn't want that part in his ear, so he had them put a new one in. He said it was expensive, *but I don't know what that means*. I just remember this being a bad experience for me. I'm not sure I learned anything from the ordeal but I know I have to be sneakier.

Another trait I seem to *"not be able to control"* is that I'm so stubborn I continue to do things my parents don't want me to. Picture on page 44 is me taking the rug out of the bathroom and bringing it into the family room. It's fun because my parents always say, *"drop it"*, or *"release"*. Then they take it and put it back. Then I do it all over again. It's fun, but I know it aggravates them.

It seems I keep finding new ways to get into trouble. My parents bought me a big king-size round bed. I like that bed because it's fluffy and soft. It won't fit into my kennel so I get to sleep next to my mom. But I get this desire to move my bed when my parents are in the bathroom. I push it, grab it with my teeth and try to drag it, and put my nose under the bed and push. It's fun, but I've also started grabbing it with my teeth and *"kneading it"* like I do with my blankets. Well, I chewed the zipper in the process of kneading and I guess my parents don't like me doing that. I can't control myself and I chew it anytime during the day that I can get to it. So now, after we get up in the morning, mom takes my new bed into the bedroom with the door shut and I don't get it again until nighttime and we're going to bed. I guess that's ok, but I'd like to chew it and drag it around. I see nothing wrong with it being my bed at night and a toy during the day. Oh well, life of a dog, especially an *"AWS"*.

I don't know much about other dogs' lives and what they do growing up, but I think because I'm a *"hunting Dog"* my instincts are different. I think I'm more inquisitive than most other breeds, and this is new to my parents. Dad says he's never had a *"hunting dog"* before and this is new to him. He's hunted behind dogs and up till now his favorite was a breed called *"German Short Hair"*. But I think I'm now his favorite.

I spend a lot of time investigating everything, and that's why my nose is in the air a lot. From the time I was a little puppy, I chased bugs and had the urge to get them into my mouth. Of course, when in my mouth, the road was not very long to my stomach. Yes, I did swallow quite a few bugs.

Then I started noticing things in our back yard. In springtime, *birds, rabbits, and lizards* all started showing up and I got the urge to start doing what I think is hunting. Now, when I go into the back yard, I immediately have to check the last places I saw those pesky animals. My dad has taught me commands like *"place"*, *"load up"*, *"sit"*, *"stay"*, *"heal"*, *"release"*, and *"**f**etch"*. Even though Dad's never had a hunting dog before, *(I believe him)* he said I should learn some of the hunting commands. He keeps trying to teach me and I keep trying to learn, and we're having fun with each other. I think I've taught him a few tricks.

Let's see, I've taught dad to go through the door before I do, be beside me when he says *"heal"* and we walk, and *"Sit"*, and feed me around 5:00am and 4:30pm, *(for the most part, he's on schedule)*. When he tells me to *"Kennel up"* and I go to the bedroom with him, he gets into his bed and goes to sleep. See dad, that wasn't so hard. Dad trains pretty easily. Moms a little harder, but she's coming around.

From the moment I came to my new home, my parents and I played a lot. Of course, we've had this **"getting acquainted"** period to initially go through and part of that is teasing each other. One tease I've always done when we're rough playing is, I bark. Well, I don't think they always like it and the more they try to make me stop, the more I do more. I heard dad tell mom it looks as if Sadie is arguing with us and talking back, just like a kid would. Sometimes, dad holds me down until I get calmer and then we go to another type of playing. I'm playing, but sometimes dad thinks it gets out of hand and puts a stop to it.

I have started stealing things, like napkins, my baby blankets, dad's underwear, socks, mom's slippers, etc. I don't steal to tear them up, but I slink around and look at mom and dad out of the corner of my eyes to see where they are and what do they know. I *"sneak"* whatever I have to *"my place"* and watch my parents until they tell me to *"release"*, and I slowly open my mouth so mom or dad can take the article out. I get into slight trouble, and it's become a game with me, except when I made the toilet paper unroll and it went all over the floor. Mom got pretty mad at me when I did that. I've only done that once.

My dog parents told us we were going to grow up and be great hunters. I don't know what that means, except I keep having these urges to do things that others I've met don't seem to do. I see pictures of the Arkansas AWS *"Red"* and he's a hunter and they always have lots of birds around him in those pictures. When I get to Arkansas to meet mom's family, I want to talk to him and ask questions about hunting and if some of these urges are hunting traits.

I can't wait to meet other AWS dogs and see how I fit in. But with the limited amount of us in the world, it's going to be hard. I haven't met any yet except when our breeder came down last winter, She brought her two AWS dogs and we seemed to get along ok, at least I thought so. I know I'm a little much for some of the older dogs to tolerate. But they have been the only AWS' I've seen.

Chapter 13

First Birthday (Finally One Year Old)

YEA.... *it's my birthday* and those are my presents in front of me. Haven't I grown? I'm supposed to be a young adult (*I'm actually a teenager*), but I don't want to grow up yet. I still want to do puppy things, (*maybe because I won't get into too much trouble if I'm still a puppy*).

Anyway, I didn't know what this day was supposed to be, but I was looking forward to it anyway. There seemed like a lot of hustle and bustle around, and that made for some excitement. Mom showed me where the presents were on the coffee table and the first thing I had to do with those presents was to *"scope"* them out. They actually smelled kinda nice because I think mom put some treats in those packages for me. You know me, I really like to eat and those packages smelled like something good.

Now I remember about presents. I got some for Christmas and that was fun. But I think I got more for my birthday than I did for Christmas. I only know counting from my dad's cousin's stairs, and it seems I have more to open than I had for Christmas. I also got some

Peanut Butter and Jelly treats and I know I'm not going to be able to have those after my birthday. My parents are concerned about my weight and to me it seems they are starving me. I'm weighed all the time and they say I'm now around 40.02 pounds. I guess that's ok, but I don't know much about weight. I do hear mom say that I have my *"girly figure back"*, whatever that is.

I did get a *special gift from dad's great grandchildren* who live in Spokane, Washington. I haven't been there yet but I think they are pretty special. In fact, I understand they are the reason for this book. The special gift was a **Bocce's Bakery Birthday Cake Dog Treats.** They are *"Peanut Butter, Carob & Vanilla Recipe"* all natural dog treats, baked in the USA. That was one of the nicest gifts I got. I know I'll get to meet them some day and I can't wait. Just maybe they'll come to see me sometime. I'd love that. They are about the same age in human years that I am in one dog year. Does that mean my life will go by faster than a humans? I don't know what to think about that yet.

Rest of the day was pretty cool. I have to say I got more treats on this one day than I have ever received on any day I can remember. I'll probably pay for that somehow. Everyone sang happy birthday to me and I felt pretty special. A good time was had by all. I finally collapsed and went to sleep on the floor and didn't wake up for the longest time.

I got a Happy Birthday hat, but I wouldn't let mom and dad put it on me. This picture is me with that hat, but I wanted to eat it so much it was only on for a couple of minutes. My parents don't know it, but the fun part was them trying to get me to wear it and my battling with them *"NOT"* to wear it. I think I won because you don't see any more pictures with it on me. The rest of my day was different than any other day. It seemed *I was pampered* more than usual and I got more treats. I know my Sunday crowd got involved with hugs and petting. So, it was pretty special. I hope I continue to have these special days because they are so much fun.

I also got a *scarf to wear that said, "Happy Birthday"*. I wore it all day. It was kind of fun because sometimes when I'm alone, I get to watch westerns on TV and this scarf reminded me of those. I think the scarfs are worn by the bad guys, and I'm sometimes a bad girl (*I have more fun that way*), so I enjoyed it. I do think *"pink"* is my color of choice, what do you think?

I know I'll have more birthdays, and I hope I have more birthday parties. This was fun. Let's see, I got special things from my parents, special gifts from great grandchildren, special hugs from the Sunday humans, and even a couple of birthday cards. I can't read, but I can tear up pretty good and I did. This was truly a great day and I want more of them.

Chapter 14

After One Year Old *(Still Fun)*

Dad asked "***Sadie, what do you think about being a year old***"? I don't quite know how or what to say about that, and I'm still having so much fun I don't want to quit being a puppy. As you can tell, I'm much bigger than 9 pounds, but I'm still just as gorgeous, and I'm pretty special. I do like the life I have; guess you can't miss something you haven't had. I think I would be a good hunter (*I hunt all sorts of bugs, birds, and lizards in the back yard*), and I have a small water feature that I probably would love to get into. Nope, I haven't been in there yet. I did catch a bird one day on our patio. I caught it when it took off to fly away, and I had to jump into the air to get it. I caught It about 2 feet into the air and carried it around in my mouth, and when I put it down to show it to mom, the dang thing flew away. Oh well, maybe I'll catch it again.

One year old and as you can see I'm still playing with my toys and having the time of my life.

I don't know where my journey takes me from here, and I don't know if this book will be continued, but if it does, it's from here on. I know I will continue to get into trouble from time to time, and I know I will want to be loved by my parents forever.

I hope those who read this can learn from this book. The responsibilities of the puppy and the human parents can be fun, but it can also be a situation where it may not be fun. We both, parents and adopted pet, must be committed to the process.

"No one likes *'parents'* who are not trained".

Authors *– Robert (Bob, Bampa) and Grandma Darbie Lee Baker.*

*Bob has two books to his credit. One was his Granddad's Diary of his first year in World War 1 entitled "**Getting To Know Granddad**", published 09-09-2009. This book chronicles Bob's Granddad Ora Bowen's diary about his day-by-day activities when fighting the Germans in **WWI**. He wrote about his trip from "Hoboken, New Jersey to Brest, France" on a converted passenger ship and his 3-day trip in a "horse Car" on a train to the front lines. The horse car had a sign inside that read "20 Horses or 40 men".*

*The second book "**I Drink My Moo, I Do My Poo, That's All I Do**", published 09-30-2020, written about his life growing up from the early 1940's to the "Pandemic". The great grandkids and beyond will get to know about their great granddad's history, Baker family history, and a little of how they got here. They can also read about some of the history of the times and what it was like growing up during that period.*

This is the first time Grandma Darbie participated in Book Preparation. She provided editing services in the two Books Bob wrote and was remarkably familiar with the subject of this book. Bob couldn't have done it without her.

Printed in the United States
by Baker & Taylor Publisher Services